YOUR KNOWLEDGE HAS VALUE

AF131032

Bibliographic information published by the German National Library:

The German National Library lists this publication in the National Bibliography; detailed bibliographic data are available on the Internet at http://dnb.dnb.de .

Imprint:

Copyright © 2013 GRIN Verlag, Open Publishing GmbH
Print and binding: Books on Demand GmbH, Norderstedt Germany
ISBN: 9783668321304

This book at GRIN:

http://www.grin.com/en/e-book/341935/to-what-extent-did-the-euthanasia-programme-contribute-to-the-gassing-of

Barbora Cervenova

To what extent did the Euthanasia Programme contribute to the gassing of Jews in extermination camps?

GRIN Publishing

GRIN - Your knowledge has value

Since its foundation in 1998, GRIN has specialized in publishing academic texts by students, college teachers and other academics as e-book and printed book. The website www.grin.com is an ideal platform for presenting term papers, final papers, scientific essays, dissertations and specialist books.

Visit us on the internet:

http://www.grin.com/

http://www.facebook.com/grincom

http://www.twitter.com/grin_com

To what extent did the Euthanasia Program contribute to gassing of Jews in extermination camps?

School: Gymnázium Jura Hronca

Word Count: 2000 excluding subheadings

Content

Section A: Plan of Investigation

The Nazi Euthanasia Program was mass murder program, predating the Final Solution by approximately two years. Its policy was not viewed as a means to mercy death; it aimed to restore the racial integrity of German nation by eliminating "life unworthy of life": individuals, who, because of psychiatric or physical disabilities represented genetic and economic burden of German society. This essay investigates: **To what extent did the Euthanasia Program contribute to gassing of Jews in extermination camps?**

The scope of research is in the years of 1939-1945. Impacts of Hitler's evolutionary ideology, economic incentives and gassing technologies will be presented. Subsequently, the essay will analyse the strengths and weaknesses of two sources: Richard Weikart's *Hitler's Ethic* and Testimony of Euthanasia survivor Friedrich Zawrel. A conclusion will then be reached based on evaluation of evidence and appraisal of the sources.

Section B: Summary of Evidence

Hitler's Evolutionary Ideology

In 1933, the Ministry of Justice released a memorandum, propos[ing] that *"it shall be made possible for physicians to end tortures of incurable patients in the interests of true humanity"*.[1] To Aryan race, these [people] were *"genetically highly defective and of inferior value to the People's Community."*[2] Getting rid of "inferior" Jews to make room for the "superior" Germans was part of the natural evolutionary process.[3] In 1940, the basis for this practice [was] that in an efficient nation there should be no room for weak and frail people.[4] Physicians may destroy life in interest of a "higher good."[5] The war provided medical professionals in conducting these murderous programmes in the name of regeneration of the Fatherland.[6] Goebbels justified this practice in his diary in 1942, writing: *"Nature is dominated by the law of struggle."*[7] Dr. Hermann Pfannmüller chose to starve [patients] to death, ridding Germany of a burden for the healthy body of [their] Volk.[8] Like those who planned physical annihilation of Jews, the planners of "euthanasia" imagined a racially pure and productive society and embraced eliminat[ion] of those who didn't fit their vision.[9] Instead, Dr. Wurm wrote in 1940: *"the feeling of legal insecurity is spreading which is regrettable from the point of view of national and state interest."*[10]

---

[1] Unknown. "Nazis Plan to Kill Incurables to End Pain; German Religious Groups Oppose Move." *New York Times.* 8th Oct. 1933. Web. 21 Nov 2013.
<http://www.life.org.nz/euthanasia/abouteuthanasia/history-euthanasia6>.

[2] Zawrel, Friedrich. Interview of Spiegelgrund Survivors. GedenkStaetteSteinhof. 2012. Web. 23 Nov 2013. <http://gedenkstaettesteinhof.at/en/interviews/videos/Friedrich-Zawrel >

[3] Weikart, Richard. *Hitler's ethic.* New York: Palgrave Macmillan, 2009. Print. pp. 194.

[4] Dr. Wurm. "Letter to Dr. Frick 5 Sept. 1940." 1940. TS. Florida Center for Instructional Technology, Florida. Web. 23 Nov 2013. <http://fcit.usf.edu/holocaust/resource/document/DocEuth.htm>

[5] Gardella, John E.. "The Cost-Effectiveness of Killing: An Overview of Nazi "Euthanasia"." *Medical Sentinel,* 4. 4 (1999): 132-135. Web. 23 Nov 2013. < http://www.jpands.org/hacienda/article21.html>

[6] Bachrach, Susan. "In the name of public health-Nazi racial hygiene." *New England Journal of Medicine,* 351. (2004): 417--419. Print. pp. 419.

[7] Goebbels, Joseph. *The Goebbels diaries.* 1942. Web. 22 Nov 2013.
<http://www.remember.org/witness/links.sp.goeb.html>

[8] Gardella, John E.. *op. cit.*

[9] "Euthanasia Program." *Ushmm.org,* 2012. Web. 1 July 2013.
<http://www.ushmm.org/wlc/en/article.php?ModuleId=10005200>.

[10] Dr. Wurm. *op. cit.*

3

Economic Incentives

If an individual was unable to be productive, his death was viewed as "humane".[11] Friedrich Zawrel's testimony shows the reality: *"I have given a few bread leftovers to a pleading person, a sick person, and this was a crime in the Third Reich."*[12] By 1945, Hitler intended the T4[13] Program to free up resources, especially money and hospital space, for the German war effort.[14] Back in 1916, the actual cost in relief for one of ["unproductive"] families was estimated at over $2,000,000 [8,400,000 RM], as there were at that time 2000 members of that socially unworthy clan.[15] In 1939, the average yearly cost for maintaining idiots has been 1,300 marks "for an unproductive purpose".[16] A statistician in the Interior Ministry wrote a report in 1941 calculating that by killing about 70,000 disabled people, the T4 program would ultimately save over 885 million marks over a ten-year period.[17] In addition, economic justification was supported by Goebbels' propaganda, manipulating the masses with posters[18], films like "I Accuse"[19] or by changing curriculum, i.e. math examples: *"The construction of a lunatic asylum costs 6 million RM. How many houses at 15,000 RM each could have been built for that amount?"*[20]

---

[11] Douglas, Pelton. *Review of Robert Proctor, Racial Hygiene: Medicine Under the Nazis.* Cambridge, Mass.: Harvard University Press, 1988. pp. 10.

[12] Zawrel, Friedrich. *op. cit.*

[13] Euthanasia Program named after Tiergartenstraße 4 in Berlin

[14] Weikart, Richard. *op. cit.* pp. 181.

[15] Robie, Theodore Russel. "Towards Race Betterment." *Birth Control Review*, XVII. 4 (1933): 93-95. Web. 21 Nov 2013. < http://www.theblaze.com/stories/2012/05/04/is-eugenics-reemerging-if-so-what-would-happen-to-these-heroes-with-special-needs/>

[16] Gardella, John E.. *op. cit.*

[17] Aly, Götz, Karl Heinz Roth, Edwin Black and Assenka Oksiloff. *The Nazi census.* Philadelphia: Temple University Press, 2004. Print. pp. 97.

[18] see appendix 1 and 2

[19] "Euthanasia in Nazi Germany - The T4 Programme | The Life Resources Charitable Trust." *Life.org.nz*, 2013. Web. 23 Nov 2013. <http://www.life.org.nz/euthanasia/abouteuthanasia/history-euthanasia6>.

[20] "Nazi Propaganda Example #1 of 4: Math Textbook Questions." *Www2.facinghistory.org*, n.d. Web. 23 Nov 2013. <http://www2.facinghistory.org/Campus/rm.nsf/61A7F88FF16FBD9585256E8E001178AC/A3F0966 ED25644E385257180005E5D71?OpenDocument>.

Gassing Facilities and Methods

In October 1939, Hitler issued "Führer decree" authorizing Reich Leader Philip Bouhler and Dr. Karl Brandt with medical killing.[21] The T4 program had served as testing ground for killing methods, and each "euthanasia" facility constructed gas chambers as the most efficient method for mass killing.[22] Brack claims that *"the patients were led to gas chamber, which they were told was a shower room,*[23] *and were killed by the doctors with carbon monoxide gas."*[24] In 1942, Hitler authorised the extension of "mercy killing" to Concentration Camps.[25] The killers in euthanasia [clinics] of Brandenburg, Grafeneck, Hartheim, Sonnenstein, Bernburg, and Hadamar also staffed the killing centers at Belzec, Sobibor and Treblinka.[26] This killing expertise of the T4 perpetrators proved useful in 1941 for the upcoming Aktion Reinhard, the mass murder of Jews.[27] Also, to facilitate the "Final Solution", gas chambers from T4 psychiatric hospitals were dismantled and shipped to Poland.[28] By 1943, there were 24 main death camps such as Dachau, Treblinka, Buchenwald, and Auschwitz engaged in ethnic cleansing [in] Concentration Camps.[29] Dr. Friedrich Menecke reported after one of his concentration camp trips that *"he had seen his former patients in Auschwitz"*.[30] Zawrel claims that even children in Spiegelgrund knew that *"the Nazis kill all the retards."*[31]

---

[21] see appendix 3

[22] Weikart, Richard. *op. cit.* pp. 188-189.

[23] Brack, Viktor. Testimony regarding gassing of insane people in Germany. Quoted in "Trials of War Criminals Before the Nuremberg Military Tribunals" - Washington, U.S Govt. Print. Off., 1949-1953, Vol. I, p. 876-886. Web. 23 Nov 2013. <http://fcit.usf.edu/holocaust/resource/document/DocEuth.htm>

[24] *ibid.*

[25] Baranowski, Shelley. *Nazi empire.* Cambridge: Cambridge University Press, 2011. Print. pp. 256.

[26] Friedlander, Henry. *The origins of Nazi genocide.* Chapel Hill: University of North Carolina Press, 1995. Print. pp. 22.

[27] Bottger, Joerg. Review of Henry Friedlander, *The Origins of Nazi Genocide: From Euthanasia to the Final Solution.* H-Holocaust, H-Net Reviews, 2000. pp. 4.

[28] Douglas, Pelton. *op. cit.* pp. 11.

[29] "Euthanasia in Nazi Germany - The T4 Programme | The Life Resources Charitable Trust." *op.cit.*

[30] Friedlander, Henry. *op. cit.* pp. 166.

[31] Zawrel, Friedrich. *op. cit.*

Section C: Evaluation of Sources

Weikart, Richard. *Hitler's ethic.* **New York: Palgrave Macmillan, 2009.**

The source was **produced** by Richard Weikart, a prominent American historian, professor at California State University and senior fellow for the Centre of Science and Culture of the Discovery Institute. Weikart has produced a number of monographs dealing with the topic, such as *From Darwin to Hitler.*

Hitler's Ethic is a secondary source, whose **purpose** is to address proper analysis and comprehensive coverage of German history. It provides historians, anthropologists and Darwinists insight into Hitler's pursue of biological improvement of human race.

The **value** of this source is in its quality and reliability. Weikart drew from a range of authentic primary sources, including Hitler's private records and unpublished German documents from Hitler's library. Moreover, Weikart is an expert on Social Darwinism and Nazi Germany, therefore this source is considered valuable.

The **limitation** of this source is the hindsight bias of 64 years that may have distorted Weikart's picture of the past since his American bias and inexperience of the Second World War provide him with no emotional connection to the event. Moreover, the book shows mainly evolutionary morality and ethics in Hitler's procedures, just a partial picture of huge Nazi complexity, not focusing enough on economy and gassing system.

Zawrel, Friedrich. Interview of Spiegelgrund Survivors. GedenkStaetteSteinhof. 2012. Web. 23 Nov 2013. <http://gedenkstaettesteinhof.at/en/interviews/videos/Fr iedrich-Zawrel >

This source's **origin** is an Austrian Friedrich Zawrel (1929), survivor of the Nazi child-euthanasia in Spiegelgrund Facility. At the time, they considered him and his parents a sick child. The interview was conducted in 2012 for Spiegelgrund victims' exhibition in Vienna.

The **purpose** is to present the most interesting facts to the public and remember the details of Euthanasia event for later generations. The interview was produced as a first hand testimony on occasion of exhibition about Spiegelgrund murders, the purpose is therefore to inform and explain the actions taking place there.

The **value** is that it is an eyewitness account from person who was part of the process, it is therefore a trustworthy source of evidence. It is a primary source that reflects Zawrel's personal experience. Considering the number of victims of euthanasia, Zawrel provides valuable information that otherwise would be lost.

The **limitation** of this source is that it is supposed to show the horrors of Nazi treatment and only testify in the area of subjective victim-perspective, it thus gives no critical view on Hitler's policy. Moreover, Zawrel was a child at the time; now he is 83, which is why his testimony was not very coherent, therefore it is hard to clearly guarantee its reliability.

Section D: Analysis

Hitler's vision of evolution and master race represented the main justifications for his intolerance toward "inferiors". Both Euthanasia Program and later Final Solution proved this to be the case. The idea of an efficient nation without weak and frail people,[32] with nature dominated by the law of struggle,[33] promised a progress, but only by eliminating the weak and unfit to live. In 1939, physicians like Dr. Pfannmüller and Brandt were ordered to end tortures of incurable patients,[34] thus preserve true humanity, "higher good" and rid Germany of a burden for healthy body of the Volk.[35] This precedent was later applied to extermination of Jews - the planners of Euthanasia imagined a racially pure and productive society embracing radical elimination of unfitting ones[36]; genetically highly defective people.[37] Yet, Euthanasia Program and war provided not only the idea, but also medical professionals in conducting these murderous programmes to regenerate the Fatherland.[38]

However, the intended perception of the benefits of disposal of the "inferior" Jews and incurables to make room for the "superior" Germans[39] was over-emphasized. Not many Nazi steps were legally justified. People felt legal insecurity, not contributing to national and state interest.[40]

Economic justification of the programme was supposed to serve as saving, leading to disposal of Jews. A means to decrease suffering was now form of cutting costs and ridding society of its "useless eaters"- death of an unproductive individual was viewed "humane".[41] However, Zawrel denies this "humanity" – it was crime to waste bread for a sick person.[42] Hitler's intention was to free up resources for German war

---

[32] Dr. Wurm. *op. cit.*

[33] Goebbels. *op. cit.*

[34] Unknown. The New York Times. *op. cit.*

[35] Gardella, John E. o*p. cit.*

[36] „Euthanasia Program." *op. cit.*

[37] Zawrel, Friedrich. op. cit.

[38] Bachrach, Susan. *op. cit.*

[39] Weikart, Richard. *op. cit.*

[40] Dr. Wurm. *op. cit.*

[41] Douglas, Pelton. *op. cit.* pp. 10.

[42] Zawrel, Friedrich. *op. cit.*

effort.[43] Back in 1916, there were only 2,000 members of that "unworthy clan" and the cost in relief for one family was estimated at 8,400,000 RM.[44] Later, professor Alfred Hoche discovered the average yearly cost for maintaining "idiots" to be 13,000 RM.[45] Furthermore, in 1941, a statistician in the Interior Ministry calculated that by killing 70,000 disabled people, program would save 885 million RM in ten years.[46] Hence, in times of unemployment and crisis this contribution seemed reasonable even though it was later not reached. However, Hitler managed to persuade people about the success of euthanasia and made use of the savings for annihilation of Jews.

Furthermore, Hitler and Goebbels used powerful propaganda for manipulating masses. They persuaded the public about burden which ill people posed, later degrading the hostile Jewish race, necessary to be exterminated. For example, in the popular film "I Accuse", a woman with multiple sclerosis was gently killed by her loving husband.[47] Posters were being published, showing the *Eradication of the Sick*[48] as a natural process and the economic burden of the sick.[49] Educational curriculum was accustomed for people to become indifferent - children's math textbooks were full of examples calculating how many life-necessities could be saved by killing.[50] Public had to acknowledge that something needs to be done to lead a satisfactory life, which proved it to be a successful method of persuasion - Hitler then continued with propaganda at a larger level with Jews.

The greatest contribution encompassed the technological advancement developed for Euthanasia. Hitler approved the killings via "Führer decree" in October 1939, allowing Dr. Brandt and Reichsleiter Bouhler to commit euthanasia.[51] The usage of gas chambers was tested and proven as the most efficient method for mass killing.[52] The selection system, method of transporting and luring were the same; told it is a

---

[43] Weikart, Richard. *op. cit.* pp. 181.

[44] Robie, Theodore Russel. *op. cit.*

[45] Gardella, John E. *op. cit.*

[46] Götz, Aly; Roth, Karl Heinz; Black, Edwin and Oksilopff, Assenka. *op. cit.* pp. 97.

[47] "Euthanasia in Nazi Germany - The T4 Programme | The Life Resources Charitable Trust."*op. cit.*

[48] see appendix 2

[49] see appendix 1

[50] "Nazi Propaganda Example #1 of 4: Math Textbook Questions." *op. cit.*

[51] see appendix 3

[52] Weikart, Richard. *op. cit.* pp. 188-189.

shower room, victims were gassed with carbon monoxide,[53] and afterwards, their corpses were processed in crematoria. Second, the physicians-killers of clinics in Brandenburg, Grafeneck, Hartheim, Sonnenstein, Bernburg and Hadamar also staffed the killing camps at Belzec, Sobibor and Treblinka[54] and their expertise proved useful for Aktion Reinhard[55] – the mass murder of Jews in the three camps. Hitler's extension of euthanasia to concentration camps in 1942[56] facilitated the Final Solution since both staff and gas chambers from T4 hospitals were sent east.[57]

By 1943, there were 24 main death camps throughout Germany[58] engaged in ethnic cleansing in Camps.[59] Indeed, fact that physician Menecke *"had seen his former patients in Auschwitz"*[60], proves the connection between these two murder programs. However, although Euthanasia Program was top secret, Zawrel's testimony suggests its vulnerability; even the children knew that *"Nazis kill all the retards"*.[61]

---

[53] Brack,Viktor. *op. cit.*

[54] Friedlander, Henry. *op. cit.* pp. 22.

[55] Bottger, Joerg. *op. cit.* pp. 4.

[56] Baranowski, Shelley. *op. cit.* pp. 256.

[57] Douglas, Pelton. *op. cit.* pp.. 11.

[58] such as Dachau, Treblinka, Buchenwald and Auschwitz.

[59] "Euthanasia in Nazi Germany - The T4 Programme | The Life Resources Charitable Trust."*op. cit.*

[60] Friedlander, Henry. op. cit. pp. 166.

[61] Zawrel, Friedrich. *op. cit.*

Section E: Conclusion

Having analysed the sources, this historical investigation came to the point that Hitler's Euthanasia Program contributed to the Final Solution by justification of murder with appealing to evolution and regeneration of Fatherland; it served as saving by cutting costs and freeing up resources, leading to annihilation of Jews; contributed to public acknowledgement of Euthanasia with propaganda, later used against Jews; the selection system, transport, luring method and killing technique served as model for gassing of Jews in extermination camps in Poland, where physicians from Euthanasia clinics staffed the killing centres. However, it may be said that the intended benefits of the programs were over-emphasized, since people felt insecure and the Program was vulnerable - it was top secret, but even children knew about it. However, the extent by which the Euthanasia Program contributed to the gassing of Jews in Extermination Camps is very large and it can doubtlessly be said that if it wasn't for this program, the annihilation of Jews would not achieve such immense measures.

Total Word Count: 2000 excluding subheadings

Section F: List of Sources

Primary Sources

1. Brack. Viktor. "Testimony regarding gassing of insane people in Germany." Quoted in "Trials of War Criminals Before the Nuremberg Military Tribunals" - Washington, U.S Govt. Print. Off., 1949-1953, Vol. I, p. 876-886. Web. 23 Nov 2013. <http://fcit.usf.edu/holocaust/resource/document/DocEuth.htm>

2. Dr. Wurm. "Letter to Dr. Frick 5 Sept. 1940." 1940. TS. Florida Center for Instructional Technology, Florida. Web. 23 Nov 2013. <http://fcit.usf.edu/holocaust/resource/document/DocEuth.htm>

3. Goebbels, Joseph. *The Goebbels diaries*. 1942. Web. 22 Nov 2013. <http://www.remember.org/witness/links.sp.goeb.html>

4. Hitler, Adolf. "Letter to Reichsleiter Bouhler and Dr. Brandt" 1 Sept. 1939." Online Handbuch, Inklusion als Menschenrecht. Web. 23 Nov 2013. <http://www.inklusion-als-menschenrecht.de/nationalsozialismus/materialien/ behinderung-krankheit-und-euthanasie-im-nationalsozialismus/euthanasie- aktion-t4/>

5. "Nazi Propaganda Example #1 of 4: Math Textbook Questions." *Www2.facinghistory.org*, n.d. Web. 23 Nov 2013. <http://www2.facinghistory.org/Campus/rm.nsf/61A7F88FF16FBD9585256E 8E001178AC/A3F0966ED25644E385257180005E5D71?OpenDocument>.

6. Robie, Theodore Russel. "Towards Race Betterment." *Birth Control Review*, XVII. 4 (1933): 93-95. Web. 21 Nov 2013. < http://www.theblaze.com/stories/2012/05/04/is-eugenics-reemerging-if-so- what-would-happen-to-these-heroes-with-special-needs/>

7. Unknown. "Nazis Plan to Kill Incurables to End Pain; German Religious Groups Oppose Move." *New York Times*. 8th Oct. 1933. Web. 21 Nov 2013. <http://www.life.org.nz/euthanasia/abouteuthanasia/history-euthanasia6>.

8. Volk und Rasse, Illustrierte Monatszeitschrift für deutsches Volkstum10.. *You Also Bear the Burden! - a hereditarily ill person costs 50,000 reichsmarks on average up to the age of sixty*. Digital image. 1936. Web. 1 July 2013 <http://www.celle-im-nationalsozialismus.de/stadtrundgang/erbgesundheits obergericht>

9. Zawrel, Friedrich. Interview of Spiegelgrund Survivors. GedenkStaetteSteinhof. 2012. Web. 23 Nov 2013. <http://gedenkstaettesteinhof.at/en/interviews/videos/Friedrich-Zawrel >

Secondary Sources

10. Aly, Götz, Karl Heinz Roth, Edwin Black and Assenka Oksiloff. *The Nazi census*. Philadelphia: Temple University Press, 2004. Print.

11. Bachrach, Susan. "In the name of public health-Nazi racial hygiene." *New England Journal of Medicine*, 351. (2004): 417-419. Print.

12. Baranowski, Shelley. *Nazi empire*. Cambridge: Cambridge University Press, 2011. Print.

13. Bottger, Joerg. Review of Henry Friedlander, *The Origins of Nazi Genocide: From Euthanasia to the Final Solution*. H-Holocaust, H-Net Reviews, 2000.

14. Douglas, Pelton. Review of Robert Proctor*, Racial Hygiene: Medicine Under the Nazis*. Cambridge, Mass.: Harvard University Press, 1988.

15. "Euthanasia in Nazi Germany - The T4 Programme | The Life Resources Charitable Trust." *Life.org.nz*, 2013. Web. 23 Nov 2013. <http://www.life.org.nz/euthanasia/abouteuthanasia/history-euthanasia6>.

16. "Euthanasia Program." *Ushmm.org*, 2012. Web. 1 July 2013. <http://www.ushmm.org/wlc/en/article.php?ModuleId=10005200>.

17. Friedlander, Henry. *The origins of Nazi genocide*. Chapel Hill: University of North Carolina Press, 1995. Print.

18. Gardella, John E. "The Cost-Effectiveness of Killing: An Overview of Nazi "Euthanasia"." *Medical Sentinel*, 4. 4 (1999): 132-135. Web. 23 Nov 2013. < http://www.jpands.org/hacienda/article21.html>

19. Weikart, Richard. *Hitler's ethic*. New York: Palgrave Macmillan, 2009. Print.

Appendix 1

(Image has been removed for publication. It can be found at:
http://www.celle-im-nationalsozialismus.de/sites/default/files/
imagecache/station_normal/10_1_Erbgesundheitsobergeri.jpg)

Source:

Volk und Rasse, Illustrierte Monatszeitschrift für deutsches Volkstum10.. *You Also Bear the Burden! - a hereditarily ill person costs 50,000 reichsmarks on average up to the age of sixty.* Digital image. 1936. Web. 1 July 2013 <http://www.celle-im-nationalsozialismus.de/stadtrundgang/erbgesundheitsobergericht>

Appendix 2

Ausmerzung des Kranken und Schwachen in der Natur

„Was nicht den Anforderungen des Seins genügt, das zerbricht"

Nazi School Poster: *"Eradication of the Sick and Weak in Nature."*

Source:

Weikart, Richard. *Hitler's ethic.* New York: Palgrave Macmillan, 2009. Print. pp. 4.

Appendix 3

(Image has been removed for publication. It can be found at:
http://www.inklusion-als-menschenrecht.de/data/_migrated/
pics/Brief_Hitler_gute_Qualitaet.jpg)

Source:

Hitler, Adolf. "Letter to Reichsleiter Bouhler and Dr. Brandt authorizing medical killing." 1 Sept. 1939." Online Handbuch, Inklusion als Menschenrecht. Web. 23 Nov 2013. <http://www.inklusion-als-menschenrecht.de/nationalsozialismus/materialien/behinderung-krankheit-und-euthanasie-im-nationalsozialismus/euthanasie-aktion-t4/>